"NOTHING IS IMPOSSIBLE,"
SAID NELLIE BLY

92
B Ly
C

Library of Congress number: 89-3782

Library of Congress Cataloging in Publication Data

Carlson, Judy.
  "Nothing is impossible," Said Nellie Bly.

  (Real readers)
  1. Bly, Nellie, 1867-1922 — Juvenile literature.
2. Journalists — United States — Biography — Juvenile literature. I. Eagle, Michael, ill.
II. Title. III. Series.
PN4874.C59C37   1989   070'.92'4   [B]   89-3782
ISBN: 0-8172-3521-3

1 2 3 4 5 6 7 8 9 0   93 92 91 90 89

REAL READERS

"Nothing Is Impossible," said Nellie Bly

by Judy Carlson
illustrated by Mike Eagle

Raintree Publishers
Milwaukee

In 1885, some people said it was impossible for a woman to do any job she wanted. But Nellie Bly said, "Nothing is impossible."

Nellie was 17 then and she had seen a story in a **newspaper** called "What Girls Are Good For." The story said that no woman could be good at a job outside of the home. Nellie did not like that, and she wrote to the newspaper saying so. She wrote so well that the newspaper gave her a job.

From that time on, Nellie worked as a **reporter**. A reporter writes about the things that she sees, and the things that people tell her.

Nellie was good at her job. She went from place to place. She liked to see new things, and meet new people. She wrote about what she saw and what people said to her. People liked to read the stories Nellie wrote.

In 1888, Nellie was working as a reporter for The World, a newspaper in New York City.

One day, Nellie spoke to John Cockerill, the man who ran the newspaper. She told him about a book she had read called Around the World in 80 Days. In the book, a man goes around the world in 80 days. At that time, people did not think that someone could travel that fast. But Nellie wanted to try.

In 1888 it took a long time to travel from place to place. There were no planes then. To go across the sea, people had to travel for weeks on a ship.

On land, people took trains. Trains back then were not as fast as trains now. It could take days to get to a place on a train.

It seemed impossible then to travel around the world in less than 80 days.

At first, Mr. Cockerill did not want Nellie to try going around the world. He did not think that she could do it. But at last he said she could.

Nellie packed just one bag to take with her around the world. She did not want to wait for her bags when she went from train to train.

On November 14, 1889, at 9:40 A.M., Nellie got on a ship in New Jersey. At last she was on her way around the world!

After weeks of traveling on a ship, Nellie got to England. There, she met another reporter who worked for The World in England.

The reporter asked Nellie what she wanted to see in Europe. She said that she wanted to see one man. She wanted to see the man who wrote Around the World in 80 Days. That man was Jules Verne.

"Go see Jules Verne?" said the reporter. "That's impossible. You don't have time!"

"Nothing is impossible," said Nellie Bly.

To see Jules Verne, Nellie had to travel on a train for two days. She did not get to sleep in all that time. But at last she came to the place in France where Jules Verne had his home.

Nellie went to Jules Verne's house. She got to ask him many things and to see the place where he wrote Around the World in 80 Days.

But too soon Nellie had to leave.

"Good luck, Nellie," said Jules Verne. "I hope that you make it around the world in less than 80 days!"

Nellie hoped so, too. But it had cost her two days to go see Jules Verne. Could she make it back home in time?

Nellie made good time all the way to Hong Kong. But when she got there, a man told Nellie that another woman reporter named Elizabeth Bisland was going around the world, too.

Miss Bisland was trying to go around the world in less time than Nellie. She had left Hong Kong days before. The man said it was impossible for Nellie to get back before Miss Bisland did.

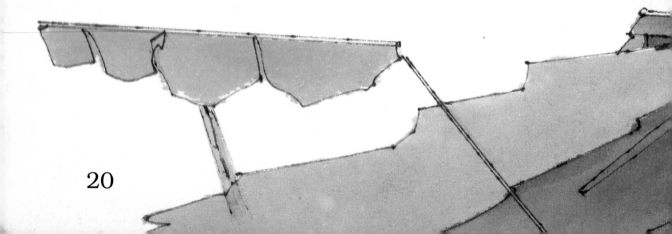

"Nothing is impossible," said Nellie. But now she didn't know. She still had a long way to go. Could she get back before Miss Bisland?

Nellie didn't give up. She took the ship across the Pacific Ocean. At last, after many weeks, she landed in San Francisco.

In San Francisco, Nellie got on a train to go to New Jersey. Nellie hoped this last trip would go fast. She could not wait to get home!

Hong Kong

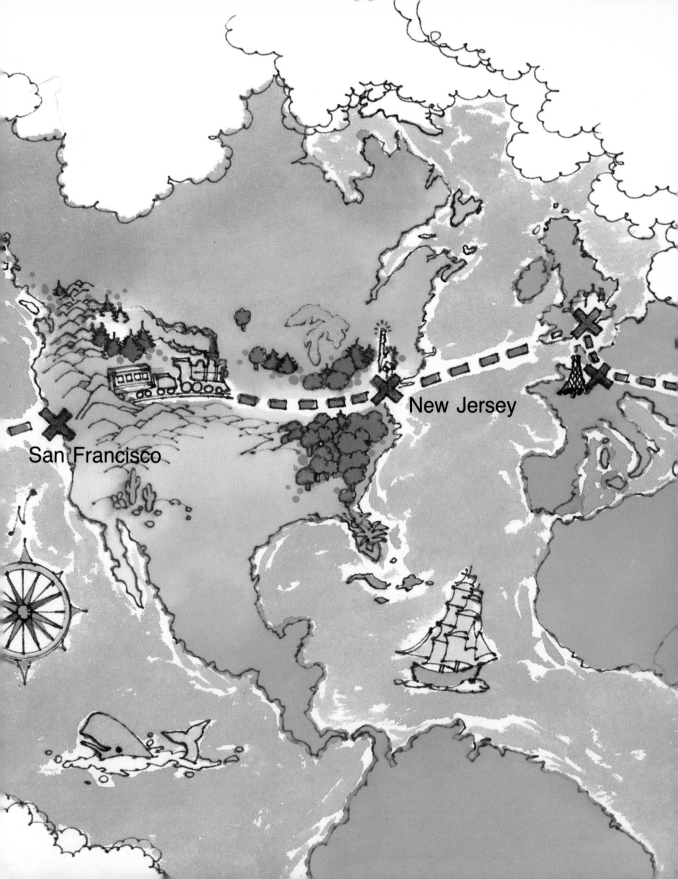

San Francisco

New Jersey

The train made many stops on the way to New Jersey. At the stops, people came to see Nellie. They had all read about her traveling around the world. They all wanted to wish her luck.

At one stop, a man yelled to her, "You must shake my hand!" When Nellie did, the man laughed and said, "I have a rabbit's foot in my hand. That will give you good luck!"

Maybe the rabbit's foot did bring good luck to Nellie. She made good time all the way to New Jersey.

Just before the last stop, Mr. Cockerill got on the train. He told Nellie that Elizabeth Bisland was not back. Nellie had come back first. Then he told Nellie to jump out of the train at the next stop. At that stop, Nellie would be back at just the place where she had left America.

As the train got to the last stop, Nellie looked out. She saw many people at the stop. They were all waiting to see her.

Nellie laughed and gave a big leap. As she landed, Mr. Cockerill looked at the time. It was January 25, 1890, 3:31 P.M., just a bit more than 72 days after she had left.

"I did it!" yelled Nellie. "Nothing is impossible! But how glad I am to be home at last!"

Nellie wrote all about her trip. She went on to write more stories, too. Her stories made the people who read them feel as if they were traveling to new places and seeing new things. Nellie showed them the world, and again and again Nellie showed them that nothing is impossible.

Sharing the Joy of Reading

Beginning readers enjoy reading books on their own. Reading a book is a worthwhile activity in and of itself for a young reader. However, a child's reading can be even more rewarding if it is shared. This sharing can enhance your child's appreciation — both of the book and of his or her own abilities.

Now that your child has read **"Nothing Is Impossible," Said Nellie Bly**, you can help extend your child's reading experience by encouraging him or her to:

- Retell the story or key concepts presented in this story in his or her own words. The retelling can be oral or written.

- Create a picture of a favorite character, event, or concept from this book.

- Express his or her own ideas and feelings about the subject of this book and other things he or she might want to know about this subject.

Here is a special activity that you and your child can do together to further extend the appreciation of this book: Nellie Bly traveled to many places during her trip around the world. Encourage your child to think about one place you have visited. Talk about how you got to the place and what you did there. Your child can also draw a picture of the place or the trip.